How I Made $100,000 My First Year as a Piano Teacher

KRISTIN K. YOST

DEDICATION

Dr. Samuel Holland - mentor, friend and visionary.
You have changed my life. Through your vision and leadership, I have been able to take my passion and turn it into a successful career, positively affecting people all over the world – students, teachers and communities alike.

CONTENTS

ACKNOWLEDGMENTS

To Dr. Rick Andrews, Dr. Donald Patterson, Mr. Alfred Mouledous, Mr. Dennis Tischhauser and Mr. Phil Scales: without you I would not have a skill set, nor would I have had once-in-a-lifetime training and experiences to get me where I am today.

To Neeki Bey: you make me want to "do better". Without your love and support, this book would still be sitting on my computer in various stages of "completion."

To my awesome parents: you're the best!

PRELUDE

Never underestimate the power of a plan. The plan may not go as you expected, but at least you had one - a guiding voice of thought, process and goals. The process of developing a business plan is what helps you think through every aspect of your business and helps you make important decisions. Kind of like life, your plan probably includes you going to school, getting a college degree, getting married, and maybe having a couple of kids. In your life, I would guess you have some semblance of a plan (though you make alterations) that guide you through big decisions.

The following pages tell my professional story from the moment I finished graduate school to where I am today. You will hear how I made a whole lot of money my first year out of school as a full-time independent music teacher, and I will give you practical advice on what I did "right", and what I would do differently to hopefully make your plan better! What you will read here are practical business suggestions and plenty of helpful advice for independent music teachers who want to make more money and who know a few financial or technological tricks, but who have never had a business or technology course to give the **confidence** to implement these ideas. Who knows, maybe you've never had one of these courses and you are fresh out of the very small (and limiting) Piano Degree box!

How I Made $100,000 My First Year as a Piano Teacher is not guaranteeing you will make six figures next year if you do all the things I discuss here, but it should help the average teacher increase his/her annual revenue by making a few simple changes or additions, and hopefully provide encouragement along the way. I want you to take all of the information you possibly can from me and use it for the greater good. I want you to be the best teacher you can be

1

and feel confident in your series of choices. I also want you to be a music teacher who is not struggling to make ends meet and living month-to-month, but instead, a music teacher who is planning for the future.

Do You Need This Book?

1. Do you have a financial plan?
2. Do you have a waiting list?
3. What are the demographics of your area?
4. Have you written a business plan?
5. Do you have a website? Please tell me you already have website. It's 2011. You HAVE to have your own website...it's like having your own telephone number these days.
6. Do you have an operating budget planned out for two years in the future?
7. Do you think that, by buying this book, you will make more money?

If you have answered NO or "I am not sure" to two or more of the questions above, you **need** to buy this book. If you answered YES to two or more questions above, you're on the right track, but are you doing all that you can to maximize your income?

Like most people, upon entering college I wasn't particularly concerned about life after a degree. I just knew I needed to get through the classes in order to have the diploma. The diploma was going to make me money although I wasn't exactly sure how. However, by my junior year I was increasingly concerned about my financial future, and after a brief period of panic (as an undergraduate student in the process of earning a music degree who wouldn't be panicking just a little bit? I decided it was in my best interest to pursue a master's degree (or maybe it was because I wanted to procrastinate that whole 'real life' thing). Either way, the decision had been made and I was bound for Dallas to work on a master's degree.

In August of 2004 I packed up my little Saturn coupe with all of my worldly belongings and drove from Eau Claire, Wisconsin, to Dallas, Texas. I was entering Southern Methodist University's Piano Performance and Pedagogy M.M. program. My first year as a graduate student was exciting, and exhausting. All I thought about was how to perfect my own piano performance and how to be a better piano teacher. It was bliss! I was learning all about piano repertoire for pre-college students, I was learning about beginner technique (who would have thought it was so important?), how the libraries worked, and how to give master-classes. That, and I was

2

studying piano with one of the most incredible teachers in the country, Alfred Mouledous. I was loving every minute of my new post B.A. student life. As wonderful as it was, I still had no idea how I was going to make a living as an independent musician (more specifically, as a piano teacher), without financial support from someone else.

It wasn't until a pedagogy course during my second year at SMU that I was completely convinced I could make a **sustainable** living on my own. My prospects looked better with, than without the M.M. As an undergraduate music major at the University of Wisconsin-Eau Claire, I studied how to analyze, perform and love music, but I did not specifically pick up how to teach little fingers to play nor did I learn how to run a business. From both UW- Eau Claire and Southern Methodist University, I picked up business tidbits, yes, but I lacked coherence in the interrelated strategic elements that running a private music studio demanded.

Plan a brochure or website as if you were taking your independent
studio to the next level.
What would you name your business?
Where would you re-locate? Why?
What tasks would you delete?

That one pivotal point in my career? An assignment for my pedagogy class: to create a brochure of my independent teaching studio. This got me thinking...what **exactly** was I planning to do once I finished in six months? Sure, teach piano...but where? How? Where would I find the students? Would I work for a school or lesson center? If I taught independently, how can I afford to buy a piano?! After the panic subsided and my heart rate returned to normal, I began to focus my attention on an idea. Instead of the traditional "insert name here" Piano Studio, I decided I needed a concept more than simply a name, and I wanted something that could grow over time. I settled on *Musical Mind Piano Studio*, which has evolved into the *Centre for Musical Minds* - what I consider my greatest accomplishment, and of which I am most proud.

> Daydreaming about
> your business is
> actually strategizing.

The way I prepared for this pedagogy class project, anyone would have though someone's life depended on it (like mine) because I was so passionate. Every day I walked my dog for more than an hour, all the while thinking of the various scenarios and possibilities. Looking back, I realize I was strategizing, but at the time I didn't realize it. To this day I cannot remember being more excited to do any homework assignment in my entire life. The process of creating my very own music studio was fascinating and thrilling to me. I went crazy! In fact, the only other extended period in my life have I ever been so excited was when I was planning the actual brick-and-mortar realization of that brochure: my own *Centre for Musical Minds*. Can you tell I have an entrepreneurial spirit? I love to create and refine BIG ideas.

Fast forward to November 2005 - just a few weeks after I began thinking about my final project for Pedagogy class. To this day I cannot remember why I decided to hire a graphic designer, or how I even came up with the idea - remember I'm just a college music student with no clue about running a business. I suppose the most likely scenario was because I became frustrated with trying to design something myself.

I was able to hire a graphic designer to design my logo, and I had 500 business cards printed, thanks to a promotion on VistaPrint.com. Using the latest publishing program ($100), I designed my own brochures, My best friend took some professional photos for my promotional materials. To top it all off, I spent $500 to get my website up and running, the best investment of all. My mother was working for the local internet company and she referred me to an acquaintance to build my website. I just needed something clean, simple and representative of what people can expect if they want to study piano with me. I received so many compliments on my website! I obviously ended up with a professional-looking product which contained the following information: teaching philosophy, bio, a few photos, CV, and contact information.

Checklist for **Marketing**

1. Logo
2. Professional looking photos
3. Website up and running
4. Business cards printed

Checklist for **Website**

1. Philosophy
2. Bio
3. Photos
4. CV/Resume
5. Contact Info

By the time I had my website, I still did not have a location for my studio, but through detailed research, I was at least able to narrow down my zip code possibilities. Before I moved, I even had three students lined up!

This brings me to my dilemma and ultimately the defining reason I was able to earn so much in such a short time. **Location, location, location.** Never underestimate the power of a zip code! I liked the Dallas area and especially liked the quality of life which offers a lower cost of living than many metropolitan areas in the country. Moving back to South Dakota or Wisconsin would mean minimal students and less than half of what I could charge here. Staying in the Dallas area seemed like the logical thing to do. I knew teaching in an apartment was out of the question for two primary reasons; sound that would bother neighbors but, more importantly, most parents seeking quality music instruction would not bring their children to an apartment for music lessons, and especially not on a keyboard. The walks began to pay off! My intermediate goal was to make a case for my parents to buy or co-sign on a house in Texas so that I could earn my living as a respectable, independent music teacher from that house.

This next part is purely cause and effect. I did my research, and I was on a mission to help others see what a wonderful world music really is. Through my journey at SMU in the master's program, I learned so much about who I am, who I am not and what I stand for -- as a person, a musician, a professional, an entrepreneur and everything else. From this I was able to articulate what I believe music lessons should be. In turn, I was able to communicate what I needed, why I needed it and what it would do for me. This clarity was the backbone for my 'big leap' into the multifaceted world of independent music education. What I was about to offer at *Musical Minds Piano Studio* was my best . That confidence alone attracted so many people to my studio. I worked extremely hard; working my way up from being a big fish in a small pond to being a big fish in a big pond.

After teaching for almost two years out of my house (2006-8) through my company *Musical Mind Piano Studio*, I was booked solid with more than 70 students. Despite a full calendar, I was tired of being a lone ranger without colleagues. I wanted to be a part of something bigger. That and I was especially tired of having to keep everything clean ALL the time! I needed the personal space separation that allowed me to just be "at home." I loved what I did out of my home; I just needed to move that love to a studio space that would add colleagues, build a team and still offer the best musical instruction I had within me. Can you tell I love what I do?

> When it's time to move your business out of your house...
>
> 1. Miss having colleagues
> 2. Need separation from business and personal
> 3. When you are tired of cleaning because of "other" people

Ultimately, what enabled me to create such a successful private studio right out of graduate school was a combination of the factors discussed here. Based on preliminary demographic research before I moved, I knew I was going to be living and teaching in a highly educated, high-earning suburb of Dallas. Parents in my area value education, the fun-factor and my holistic approach to music. I defined what I do best and was working to carve my niche into the marketplace.

Demographic research = salary increase.

Highlight educated parents

High earnings

Value of Education

Value of your philosophy

In 2008 I found my ideal studio space and moved my *Musical Mind Piano Studio* into a commercial location. With the new location came a new name; I renamed it the *Centre for Musical Minds*. CMM is my vision of a great place to be not only for students, but for teachers as well. I personally feel the *Centre for Musical Minds* is one of the nation's most innovative centers for music study, in particular piano study. We serve the community by offering the highest standard of musical excellence where teachers, students and young artists all thrive under one roof. Beginning with only piano lessons, CMM now offers a variety of programs and classes dedicated to transforming lives and enriching the community. Focusing on comprehensive music instruction and dedicated to lifelong learning, we offer private lessons in piano, guitar and voice, we offer Musikgarten for little ones, and Piano for Pre-K. Recently we added a Recreational Music-Making component as well as an Online Lesson department. It's an exciting place!

Centre for Musical Minds

My logo, the pride and joy that resulted out of my **plan.**

> **Be willing to expand your services!**
>
> The Centre began with piano lessons and has expanded into guitar, voice, Musikgarten, Piano for Pre-K, Recreational Music-Making, African drumming, song-writing, camps, technology sessions and Online Lessons. Take the interests of your community and run with them!

CMM offers song-writing, African Drumming, all kinds of camps and technology sessions for kids and somehow we manage to find time to have six performances each year. One favorite annual event is when I hire a rhythm section to accompany the students. I call it a Keyboard Jam, but it's really a recital that has been redefined. The students are "restricted" to playing in a pop, country, rock or jazz style throughout, as we want them to make use of the opportunity to play with a drummer, bass player, keyboard player and guitar player.

As you will read, there are many variables that go into earning a six figure income, but ultimately you have to believe in what you do, take what you do seriously, and enjoy instilling a love for music into your students. Your ideas have to be bigger than yourself. Most importantly, never underestimate a strategy. With an underlying philosophy in place, some logistical factors sorted out and a space where people WANT to be - you're on the right path to earning your six-figure income!

2 – PRODUCT

Do you teach your instrument? Or do you teach music? Too often, musicians teach private music lessons, without regard to "music", but rather they get caught up in technique, or in teaching a specific piece, or in preparing for a theory exam. We're all guilty of it sometimes, but it's what you do consistently that determines your product. In the lessons you teach, do you transfer the art of music into the art of teaching? Do you care so much about scales and technique that you neglect popular music because the "core repertoire" is consuming 100% of the lesson? Welcome to 2011, popular music IS part of the core repertoire.

Where you live will dictate the value system of the people in your community. The community I chose to begin my career is well-educated and has disposable income. In Chapter 6, I will address the importance of demographics and what to seek to determine your earning potential.

The kind of students I attract (and the parents who finance their musical education) are often not interested in classical competitions but are more interested in learning about music as a hobby. However, they treat it as a serious hobby and they want to excel at it. This hobby allows them to learn the discipline while having fun and playing music they recognize and enjoy. My students are **required** to study popular music, read chord chards, improvise, perform in recitals and take theory evaluations based on their level of understanding. (I wrote the evaluations myself). I also have about 25% of my student base that participate in The Achievement Program, endorsed by Carnegie hall.

> Match your teaching to your parents' and students' wants. My students are not interested in a strictly classical background, but they do treat their music education as a serious hobby and they want to excel.

You can see that I have a mix of parents and students wanting education blended with "fun." The common denominator in both sets however, is that they understand and enjoy what the students play. For me to accept a student who only wants to play Western Classical music would be a detriment to the student and the parents, as well as painful for me. It would be the recipe for unhappiness for everyone involved!

Sample 30-minute Lesson Plan
5' Flash Class or Rhythm game on the iPad
5' Review of theory assignment
10' Play pieces from week before, and begin new
- What fun activities can you incorporate to make the music come to life?
5' Technical work
5' Popular music with track or Harpsichord setting for Baroque piece

When deciding what you value in your teaching content, ultimately there are just not enough hours to get through the material you would like each week, but there is certainly enough time (with the proper planning), to get through the material you value for your students and their course of study. Plan the time and activities accordingly. For each student, I would hope the allotment of time and pieces is different. Catering to each student involves meticulous and forward thinking, planning and implementation all within a very tight timeframe. Good teaching is not having a formula that you apply to Sally, Dylan and George all in the same way. Good (and effective) teaching is having a knowledge base of **what** works, and **when** to use it. I will never forget the lesson I learned in pedagogy:

"80% of what great teachers do is choose the right music and give it at the right time." Thank you Samuel Holland!

For a teacher to draw in large numbers of a certain "type" of student, the teacher should exhibit characteristics of a strong parent and leader. This means you need to articulate your strengths and capabilities and recognize your limitations. Although I feel very strongly about incorporating 'popular music' in the core repertoire, if you are morally opposed to it, you need to make it known to your potential clients up front. Ultimately you need to be supportive of the student who enters the talent show with Linus and Lucy, (even though you would rather be teaching them a Clementi Sonatina). A strong leader knows how to guide in the 'right' way while still maintaining a standard.

Sheer Numbers

The work involved in setting up a life that earns six figures annually is not a very realistic lifestyle that teaches 25 students per week. However, let me also state that there are a couple teachers who can charge $100 an hour in certain zip codes. For the rest of us, if my salary benchmark is your dream or goal, take what I say to heart: wake up and take a close look at your reality.

Doctors	Attorneys	Business Executives	Piano Teachers
High stress	High Stress	High Stress	Low/Medium Stress
250k average annual salary	150k average annual salary	100-250k average annual salary	Yours?
60+ hour work weeks	60+ hour work weeks	60+ hour work weeks	30-50 hour work weeks
High job satisfaction	Medium job satisfaction	Medium job satisfaction	High job satisfaction

The life of an independent music teacher typically does not include high amounts of stress all the time, but it does require incredible planning, patience and a lot of psychology, for students and their parents! This and an occasional 50-60 hour workweek. The romantic notion of sitting next to a wonderful piano student all day, sipping an iced tea in a room with an ocean view is not very realistic, but you can have a pleasant studio with students whom you have interviewed and whom you now enjoy, sipping an iced tea in a room with a view.

3 - MODERN THINKING

> Embrace the times in
> which we live! Use
> Garage Band to practice
> scales...you know,
> there's an app for that.

I have always embraced things that are current. Not trendy, but current. If I'm not having fun, I don't typically choose to be a part of something. As a self-proclaimed gadget girl, it is important to me to keep up with what my students' listening tastes; it gives me cues as to their musical influences and to their use of spare time. I am a firm believer in embracing the times in which we live. Yes, I still teach scales and Baroque Minuets, but I also teach pop chart reading and incorporate Garage Band. I use my iPod/YouTube whenever I have the chance to make a lasting impression. We live in an ever changing world that requires us to evolve faster than ever before – and there is SO much information at our fingertips.

To attract and sustain relationships with students and parents, a successful teacher needs to be able to communicate on a level that is not intimidating, and that embraces student interests. Remember, we always have a choice: do we want to go down to the level of a third grader, or do we want to bring them up? I would hope the answer to that question would be to bring them up to our level, but with that answer comes the responsibility and the ability to communicate and be understood by the person(s) you want to influence. In the case of the teacher-student relationship, you need to make sure the parents are also on board.

I had a student who studied with me for three years, who is by all definitions a "prodigy." He just turned eight, is in high school classes, reads advanced literature with ease and can analyze a Mozart sonata in about ten minutes. His biggest musical challenge is feeling rhythm. I am not talking about the scientific breakdown of the dots on the page here, I am talking about the actual feeling of a steady rhythmic pulse. What better way to learn how to "feel" the music than to play Guitar Hero or play along with a loop via an iPad or computer? The loop will force my student to use steady rhythm, to practice syncopations and to have fun!

Scales with a backbeat (in GarageBand for example) are so much more fun than a ticking metronome, don't you think?

I'll take a Frozen Ape please!
Instead of a droning
metronome, use iPad apps
like Music flash Class,
FunkBox and more.

I use the iPad for its *Music Flash Class,* which is an incredible app, *FunkBox,* *ReadRhythm* and *Frozen Ape Tempo* (metronome app). I also recently discovered *ClassicalGuitar* where I can play chord changes along with my student. It's awesome!

Again, Your Product

Some of you are going to agree with me, and some of you are not. I truly feel we are doing our students a disservice by only teaching western classical (standard) repertoire with two performances per year on a stage with an audience who would rather be having their eyebrows waxed. Let's face it, they really only want to hear their kid play and if they had the choice, they would get up and leave. Historically, music did not originate on a concert stage, so why do pianists and piano teachers value the traditional recital format so much? Is it really that important if a student plays their memorized piece on a stage with people staring at them like they are a zoo animal? Wee, look at me!

What about if we instead made it more about the music rather than the musician. Am I saying we should abandon Bach Inventions and Beethoven Sonatas? No, but I am saying we need to embrace the Top 40 radio hits and encourage student compositions.

If Bach and Beethoven were alive today, they wouldn't be playing Bach and Beethoven; they would be making music with other people, creating their own voice and reaching out to the general population. This is a common thread in music history forgotten or neglected by the highly educated.

What's the point of having a skill used only on a concert stage? My friend Kathy Cordeiro has coined this the "trained monkey" syndrome, and it's true! You can train a child to imitate anything, but that is not the point of education. The point of music education, I would hope, is to nurture a student's desire to learn a musical instrument, raise a level of cultural awareness, provide memorable and enjoyable life experiences and to encourage communication in various mediums. Teaching how to make dots and symbols come alive is no small feat!

As far as "recitals" are concerned, the best $600 investment I make each year is when I hire a live rhythm section to play with the students for a "Keyboard Jam," the event I mentioned earlier in this book. Parents will happily pay a $15 fee to cover the costs of the live musicians so don't use cost as a prohibiting factor to make music come alive. This rhythm section needs to be professional musician friends who can follow anyone and play anything at any time (and let me tell you, there can be some interesting rhythms and beats going on at the piano!) I have never received so many compliments and positive comments about any other recital format. "I wish my piano teacher would have done that for me when I was a kid." "That was so cool!" "Thanks Miss Kristin, today was the first time I actually felt like a REAL musician." These are meaningful life experiences which will last a lifetime. And when given the chance in 10-15 years, I will bet these students will be more apt to support live music. That is when I will know my job as a music teacher has been done, and done well.

Your Beliefs
In graduate school I had to 'fight with,' for lack of a better word choice, people who thought I was less of a teacher because I did not value Sonatinas above Star Wars. In my mind, the styles are one and the same: they are both examples of 'good' music. Not only was I being challenged intellectually, I was being forced to create my own opinion, based on my own beliefs. At the time I felt bad but, as I look back, so much good came out of that experience! By being forced to think for myself, I was able to articulate what

14

I believe, and I figured out my own ways to achieve "good" sound. Drum roll please...I was becoming an independent learner.

Your Tools

For the majority of the population, to make money and to be a marketable music teacher, you need to be at least semi-up-to-date with your teaching gadgets. You don't have to be Twittering on an hourly basis, or checking your students' Facebook walls ALL the time, but you do need to have a few core products.

Music teacher checklist of technology gadgets and websites you MUST have:

- Internet Access in your studio
- YouTube.com bookmarked
- iTunes - EVERYONE has this, you should too
- Keyboard with MIDI capability (doesn't have to be expensive)
- MIDI USB - to connect your keyboard to your computer
- Garage Band (Mac) or Audacity (PC)
- Good sound system/External speakers

Modern Piano Teacher as Entrepreneur
First published for ComposeCreate.com Spring 2011

What does it mean to be **modern** anyway? What comes to my mind are concrete floors, white walls and uncomfortable chairs. I suppose this is directly related to museums (of modern art) but on a practical piano-teacher level, to me it means someone who isn't old-fashioned. The modern teacher doesn't negate standard classical repertoire, of course, but the modern teacher does embrace music coming from neighborhood basement bands, traditional African melodies, and that crazy new "indie" stuff heard in coffeehouses.

For a piano teacher to be considered "modern" in a musical sense, I use the following criteria:

1. *Multi-culturalism* - the teacher embraces many backgrounds and musical tastes in lessons. Teaching music from other countries develops an appreciation for good music in ALL forms. Recently I had the privilege of writing pedagogical commentary for a new series, (www.PianoAccents.com) and am thoroughly convinced it is our responsibility as piano teachers to make music from all over the globe come alive, not just music from western Europe.

2. *Popular Music.* Teach current music heard on the radio that can be recognized by 7-10 year olds. Sorry everyone, the Beatles are not considered 'popular music' anymore. "The Rose"? It's beautiful, but the kids have no idea what it is or which movie from which it originated. I have had to come to terms recently with *The Lion King* being labeled as "old." I absolutely LOVE Mona Rejino's arrangements for intermediate students that appear in 'Current Hits', and Wendy Steven's new book, "Contemporary Pop Hits", both published by Hal Leonard. Often times I go on www.MusicNotes.com and print music from there - then simplify and arrange at home. Take it a step further and just view it on your iPad!

3. *Apple Phenomenon.* There is a small "i" in front of all of my favorite things, or so it seems. The teacher must be able to identify and know what an iPod is, and know some great music teaching apps! The teacher is definitely modern if he/she actually uses an iPod, iPad or other fun gadgets during the lessons. No, a metronome is not a gadget. Fact of the matter is CD's are basically out-of-date now. iTunes has transformed our lives into a digital music world with endless possibilities. At the very least, you need to be able to meet your student halfway with their technology capabilities. iTunes and Apple continue to enhance my life.

Modern in the financial sense of being a piano teacher means being an entrepreneur. You need to have the mindset that your job title is "CEO of My Own Company." According to Wikipedia, an entrepreneur is defined as "one who undertakes innovations, finance and business acumen in an effort to transform innovations into economic goods." This Wikipedia explains that entrepreneurship may mean a completely new organization or it may mean revitalizing mature organizations in the face of a grand opportunity. Many of us think of entrepreneurship as that first option, the one of starting new businesses (referred as Startup Company); but entrepreneurship's definition has been expanded to include social and political forms of entrepreneurial activity. Basically, you and I are revitalizing a mature organization (piano instruction has been around for a while), creating a business model that makes its practitioners money. Sink or swim? If you choose the swim option, just remember it requires an enormous amount of knowledge and work.

So how do the terms "modern", "piano teacher" and "entrepreneur" fit in the same sentence? As a private piano teacher, you wear several different hats and therefore have a significant amount of accountability to a lot of people. Strictly speaking though, you are a person who is taking on a risk of financially supporting yourself and possibly your family by teaching piano lessons for your income. You are building your brand (your company's or your own name). As an entrepreneur you have planned your business, you have calculated the risk, done some demographic assessment, purchased the necessary equipment, earned your education, credentials and even have a fabulous website.

As an entrepreneur, piano teachers have a marketing hat, a branding hat, an IT department hat, a customer service hat, an accounting hat and even a teacher hat! So many hats, so little time. As a teacher, you have so much knowledge, from pedagogical literature to philosophy, but you also need to have the knowledge about how to run a business, particularly a successful one. One of my favorite websites for practical information regarding a wide range of business topics is www.hbr.org (Harvard Business Review).

In order to be a successful entrepreneur, you need to brush up on leadership skills, marketing and advertising, and certainly on accounting. For accounting, I am under the assumption everyone is using QuickBooks, as it is hands-down the most popular accounting software on the market. You will need to have a business plan, a budget, and ultimately a short term set of goals that leads to a long-term set of goals. How in the world can you turn all of this hat-swapping into something meaningful in your life? You can start by creating a budget. List all of your monthly expenses and income from the previous year. Where are you now? Where do you want to be financially? Have a plan! Once your budget is together, work on your financial goals and create a plan to make those goals a reality.

The Modern Piano Teacher is an entrepreneur by definition, regardless of resisting opinions from practitioners, educators, veteran instructors or first-year tutors. Young doesn't mean modern and old doesn't mean traditional...what piano teachers need to do is unite. Raise the level of playing in popular music. Raise the level of tuition awareness and piano teacher's salaries. Bring music from non-western cultures into the core of classical curriculums.

Your life is a performance. When you learn a recital program you take it one movement, one piece at a time and envision what the end product will be like for the performance. You probably plan what you are going to wear ahead of time, arrange all of the non-musical details, and then hopefully celebrate once you have achieved your goal. You are the piano teacher and you are the entrepreneur - one project at a time.

The Importance of World Music at the Piano
First published for ComposeCreate.com Spring 2011

You listen to music all the time, whether you realize it or not. In stores, in restaurants, on your iPod, in the elevator, and on TV. Turn on the radio and there's old country, new (pop) country, rock, R&B, pop, a public radio station with classical music and news, or talk radio. If you live in the southern United States, chances are there are some Spanish-speaking stations that play Tejano music. My guess is, if you are like me, you keep going back to the same stations, with the same artists, which plays the same type of music, which in turn plays into what you value. As a music teacher, do you question why it matters the type of music we educators reveal to our students?

As a piano teacher, I am somewhat ashamed to admit that I rarely choose to listen to piano music when I'm in the car, running, or out and about. However, in my defense it doesn't give me the "boost" or motivation that I get when I listen to (yes, here it is!), country music or Top 40 hits. I LOVE popular music, even though I have spent thousands of hours 'perfecting' my classical background. I love a good driving rhythm and 3 minutes and 30 seconds of unadulterated fun. If Beethoven had an iPod, to what do you think he would be listening?

The reality is that the job of Western-Classically trained piano instructors is to create, facilitate and expose students to as many positive musical experiences as can fit in a music education. This includes -- but is not exclusive to -- music teacher organization festivals, recitals, group classes, history, theory, holiday music, live music in the community and WORLD MUSIC. Yes, this means your students need to **hear** music from different parts of the world, not just Western Europe or America. Can you imagine being able to experience and hear African drumming as a child, and learning about a completely different culture? Or sounds from India - learning about the instruments and tuning systems? It may not be your students' favorite subject, but who knows - it may turn out to be a passion they follow closely for the rest of their life! The message to send to students with Indian heritage speaks loud and clear: your value system reaches past Germany and Italy. Imagine how much less of a judgmental a society can be if music and cultural norms aren't simply judged as "oh I don't like that kind of music," but rather enjoyed and appreciated for what they are. Your students may never choose to turn on a recording of music from Brazil, but at least they will appreciate it and not complain when they are at a South American restaurant and they aren't hearing American Pop in the background. (Let's hope they don't order a hamburger either...)

This past winter I had the privilege of providing pedagogical commentary for Neeki Bey's first book in his new series, *Piano Accents: Africa*. The book consists of ten African pop and folk songs that he found most meaningful to him, and that he thinks students will enjoy playing at the piano. The zenith of the book is the corresponding accompaniment tracks; the whole village comes out to make music! Each song has three tracks: slow, mid and performance speeds. In the book I tell the students to avoid counting but, rather, to listen, feel the groove and find the articulations using their ears and eyes. Why, you ask? Because that's what the music is all about! It's not about right-or-wrong rhythms and notes...it's about the experience and, in African culture, coming together for an event such as a wedding, baby naming ceremony or family event. Two of my students' favorite songs to play are Jingle Bells and Happy Birthday...because these are songs that are familiar and sung at events that are celebratory. As world-renowned African drummer S'Ankh Rasa said at our latest African Drumming session, "I've never been to a 'concert' in Africa." Meaning, so little of what we do as music educators has anything to do with a concert stage and memorized music. Music in traditional African culture is about the larger community and special occasions - not what happens, or what does not happen on a concert stage when children are fearing for their life during a recital in which everyone wants to go eat corndogs or get their brows waxed.

In using *Piano Accents: Africa* (PianoAccents.com) with some of my students this year, I have found their acceptance to be gradual rather than immediate. "This music sounds weird" becomes "This music is so much fun" which turns into "Can we play with the track today?" Without this book and without me taking the time to value something other than Western Classical music, their lives would not have been enriched. Now, with the help of Bey's Book, I have been able to expose my students to sounds they may never have encountered. The groundwork for a more open and less judgmental society is being set, and we are all benefitting from the exposure.

I would like to challenge each and every piano teacher to choose at least one song for their students this year, which doesn't come from a Western Classical tradition or an American Pop favorite, but rather comes from a foreign land that most children experienced only in books. Take them on an excursion that goes past the United States, Western Europe and through Beethoven the Beatles and beyond.

19

4 - ORGANIZATION

I wish someone would have explained organization to me before I started my private studio; an organized workspace and the importance of record-keeping should never be underestimated. If you never read another book on organization, please treat yourself to David Allen's best-selling book, *Getting Things Done: The Art of Stress-Free Productivity*.

In addition to studying Allen's book, create a checklist of office supplies and think through an effective system of organization. Start with where you are today and then think through where you hope to be in five years. Will your filing system make sense, both now and years from now? Is it EASY to use?

Purchase a label maker that has a power adapter; that way, you can just plug in rather than always keeping working batteries. As Allen suggests, if the task takes less than two minutes, do it right then. All of the little things add up and become taxing, weighing you down. From the beginning, keep separate all bank accounts, which will make tax time much easier, and more clear. Whether you have a corporate structure such as an LLC, or a less formal DBA (Doing Business As), any financial institution will be happy to set you up with a second bank account.

There are many ways to keep track of student progress, pieces and event participation. For me, electronic files work best. Since I use a MacBook and am devoted to Apple, I use the Microsoft Office equivalent for Macs, and the word-processing program I use is called Pages. At the beginning of each year, I plan a year's worth of performance pieces for each of my students and keep that information on a spreadsheet, using Numbers (the Excel equivalent). I print that document out and post it on the back of my office door as an easy reference. This also reduces duplication of music (if any) on recitals.

> Make your performance plan...once a year. At the beginning of each school year, I plan a year's worth of performance pieces for each of my students, and keep that information readily available on a spreadsheet. I then post that document on the back of my door for easy reference.
>
> Due to careful planning, my accuracy is about 95% for hitting "the right piece, at the right time." This results in extremely low student turnover throughout the years!

As far as music is concerned, I make a VERY large order in August when I plan for the entire year's use of method books and supplemental music. I order my "student savers" that I always use, plus a few extras. When I need music in the interim, I go to the local music store – which ends up being once every few months. I find the large order in August, combined with my student planning for the year, saves time and hassle, making my life easier during the year when I am busy with other things. Of course, I am not afraid to alter the plan if needed, but due to careful planning, my accuracy is about 95% for hitting the "perfect repertoire at the perfect time."

I hire an assistant to file my receipts weekly and a bookkeeping service to enter my expenses and revenue into QuickBooks online. This constant stream of organization saves a lot of hassle and headaches come tax time and provides a quick reference, should it be necessary, at any point during the year.

Creative Time Management for the Full-time Independent Music Teacher
first published Spring 2011

Have you ever been so busy with parents, students, technology and more students that you fail to have three minutes in a row to use the restroom or pay a forgotten phone bill online? I think it's safe to say that we have ALL been there, done that and some of us still continue to commit to ridiculous hours of teaching sans breaks. Are these hours so ridiculous or are we the ones who are ridiculous?

We do this to ourselves. We create unrealistic schedules. Where in our Piano Teacher Employee Handbook does it state "teacher must not schedule fifteen minute breaks?" Or, "teacher must dehydrate so as not to 'waste' precious lesson time." I have said before, and will say it again, I have no shame in starting my Music Flash Class app, walking away while it quizzes my students for three to five minutes while I take care of business. I also don't mind starting a lesson five minutes late or ending five minutes late. Anything past ten and I start to feel bad but when nature calls or when I forget to pay a bill, Armageddon is not going to happen. However, all this could be avoided if I would just schedule a little extra time midway through my six-hour teaching day. I personally don't feel bad using the restroom while a student is warming up or practicing - should you?

If we are really doing it right, tuition dollars are going to so much more than our minute-per-minute lessons. Why do we as piano teachers feel so guilty when our students don't get all 2,700 seconds of our undivided attention?

Schedule Office Hours – like a college faculty member would!

Office Hours are something in which I also firmly believe, you know, like college faculty. I have tried to train my students and parents to respect my time, and, for the most part, it has worked! My office hours are prior to lessons starting each day (I give myself 2-3 hours) so each day is different. I post these hours on my door for all to see. I don't answer/return work phone calls unless it is during office hours. Just as I separated my location and my finances into personal and business categories, I divide my time in likewise fashion.

Do you have the chatty parent who likes to talk your ear off on a weekly basis? Sometimes I have time to chat -- and enjoy it when I do -- but other times I don't. Many parents enjoy getting to know a music teacher, but if I have something I need to complete, I make a point of saying, "I enjoyed our lesson, but I have to take care of something really quickly before my next student arrives...looking forward to hearing you next week!" I get to take care of my business and everyone leaves happy.

Two Administrative Programs I can't live without:
1. Quick Books for business reports and taxes
2. Studio Helper for scheduling, invoicing, record-keeping and rosters

To maximize my efficiency year-round, the two programs I absolutely cannot function without are Quick Books and Studio Helper. The website www.QuickBooks.com saves TONS of time when tax season rolls around, in addition to giving me a penny-for-penny analysis of the Centre for Musical Minds business accounts. The website www.StudioHelper.com saves a significant amount on administrative tasks such as scheduling, invoicing, record keeping and updated student rosters. It exports and prints beautifully. Pick up ideas on www.MusicTeachersHelper.com as well.

Another way I "manage" my communications with students and parent is to keep my website up-to-date. Parents and students can get all the information they need online. This one efficiency habit cuts down on my emailing considerably. If I do need to send out emails, Studio Helper allows me to select which group(s) of people I need to email and I can do it relatively quickly.

Remember the "two minute rule" from David Allen's *Getting Things Done: The Art of Stress-Free Productivity*: if a task can be completed in two minutes or less, do it right away. If not, put it on a "next action" list. This is much better than a to-do list because the next-action is for items that need to be completed within 24 hours. I have two separate lists: one for next-action and another with projects that have deadlines. The challenge for me is getting in the daily habit of double checking my lists - but when I do, this system works beautifully!

Creative Time Management recap:
- Schedule short breaks
- Three to five minute measurable-progress activity (e.g. Flash Class app) at the beginning of the lesson, allowing you time for a quick personal break if needed.
- Schedule Office Hours to accomplish administrative tasks
- Honor those Office Hours! You are worth it.

- Harness scheduling/accounting programs to lighten the administrative load of being an independent music educator.
- Keep a Next-Action list

5 - WEBSITE AND RANKING

To the outside world, your face is important, even if you are not directly drawing in clients. Parents, students and prospective families can learn just a little more about you, then tell their friends, who tell their friends.

I am a stickler for good websites, especially one that includes your face on it. Find a reasonable designer and pay him/her. As your primary source of income, it is well worth the price. If you would like to try a do-it-yourself website, my second favorite option is an iWeb site - they're awesome and, if you own a Mac, free. When Drs. Nancy and John Smith are looking for a piano teacher for their two children, like the majority of 30 and 40-somethings, they probably do a basic search on the internet. Several websites pop up, but yours is on the first page, and it is very nicely done. When they compare your site to other teachers with comparable education and experience, to whom do you think they will gravitate?

Once you know what you would like to call your company (yes, you are the owner of a company now), do a basic search to see if the domain is available. I personally have an account with GoDaddy.com, but there are several others that are user-friendly such as Register.com . The annual cost for owning the web address is around $10.
traffic.

> 80% of my new student business in my first year of teaching came from online traffic, NOT from personal referrals. That's $1,000 spent in the right direction!

Never underestimate the power of a website! My $500 website was from 2006, so, of course, the prices have gone up a bit. You still should be able to get a great, nicely functioning website for under $1,000. If you own a Mac, use the iWeb program. Or buy an ready-made template. Or better yet, seek out college or high school students who might do this on the side or for a class. Not only will it be less expensive, but it will most likely be up-to-date and visually appealing to your audience. When building your own site, or having someone else do it for you, be sure you can answer the following questions and be certain you are comfortable with those answers.

1. Do you offer hosting and, if so, how much on an annual basis?
2. Is this platform easy enough for an amateur to update regularly?
3. If the site needs to be updated by someone other than myself, what is the hourly rate?

How can you tell if your website is effective? Being the numbers geek that I am (and proud of it!), one of the most exciting events in my month occurs when I read my Google Analytics report and I run comparisons of hits to my website from previous months and year. When number of hits are up, I feel like I have won the lottery. When numbers are down, I think about where we are in the calendar-year and if necessary, re-evaluate the all aspects of the website and design, and I make sure I stay on top of the numbers in comparison to reports from previous years. Regardless of the numbers going up or down, I am always intrigued by who is searching, what they seek and how long they stay on the website. Because of my strategic Search-Engine-Optimization campaign this fall, I am pleased to report that my current website is now in the single best spot on the web (third entry) for the keywords I programmed on Google, and we are climbing the ranks of Bing and Yahoo. My website was on the middle of page 2 in October and within two months I was on the top of page 1 - all because of a few (free) changes I made.

Once you have your website, the next and most important step is to get it ranked on page one of Google, Chrome, Bing or Yahoo. Be sure you submit your business to the search engines. My best advice to you, and the way I was able to get www.CentreforMusicalMinds.org on Google's page one was a time-consuming but effective path. Worth the hours and frustration of doing it myself!

1. First, make a list of the search words with which you want your website to be associated.

2. Make sure those words are on your website. You can do this by using the verbiage in your message, by 'hiding' it in the background or simply by putting the phrases in the side margins.

3. Make your website relevant to the search engines; register wherever possible. E.g. Google Ad words, business profiles, Yellow Pages, Yahoo.

4. Google analytics is your best friend! It tells you what the most popular search words are, how many hits per day you get, time spent. Analyze and see where you can improve and gain more of the market.

Average costs surrounding a website

Domain - $10/yr
Hosting - $50/yr
Buildout – Free to $2,000
Maintenance – Free! You should have a platform that YOU can update, so you don't have to pay a designer after the initial start-up..

6 - DEMOGRAPHICS

> The single most important factor in allowing my income to grow into six figures? Knowing the demographics of my city! Do you know yours?

The single most important factor in allowing my income to grow into the six figures was the demographic of my city. In November and December of 2005 (just prior to my graduating), I did this research exclusively online. Music educators are a click away from building or improving their music business with savvy demographics knowledge.

How much money does an average household make? What about the median age in your city? Your city's homepage, or the United States Census website at www.census.gov will tell you. The following is a list of resources you should check out before deciding if/where you will locate or relocate your music business:
- U.S. Census
- IRS Data
- Chamber of Commerce
- Universities
- Small Business Administration
- Corporate Annual Reports
- State and local taxes
- Local Music Stores

With little reading or analyzing, here is some basic information available on my city's website (www.FriscoTexas.gov) for the year 2009.

Median Age	Median Income	Households with Children	School District	Degrees
34 y/o	$101,574	52%	37,000+ students enrolled	94%HS Grads 57% BA +

In 2009 there were 39,000 households in Frisco, with an average size of three people, so I know that families are small and likely to have more resources. One-third of the population is younger than 18. Five percent are senior citizens. The sexes are divided almost evenly, with 51% female, 49% male. More than 37,000 students were enrolled in Frisco ISD for the next (2010/2011) school year.

Of course there is more data available such as race, employment, land use breakdown, tax information, property tax values and much more. However, the three biggest factors for me were:
1. Age of city
2. Median household age
3. Median household income

Taking into consideration the research numbers from ten years prior to moving, and the city demographic projection, what music teacher wouldn't want to live here based on these numbers? It's job security; disposable income combined with a young population. Clearly education is valued and with 37,000 students enrolled in public school, there should be an ample supply of students seeking music lessons.

> I spent my time and energy highlighting my strengths and defining my niche. My time was not spent on trying to be better than my competition.

I figured if people have disposable income, I must be in good shape! Then, instead of focusing my energies on my competition and trying to be "better than" someone else, I focused my energy on highlighting my strengths and developing my craft, defining my niche and meeting other local teachers.

Realize that, in a region where the annual household income is $32,000 a year, you will not realistically be able to achieve a six-figure income based solely on private lesson teaching. That being said, let's take a look at a few simple things you **can** do within your given or potential demographic.

Market Rate
As an educated and experienced teacher, be sure your rate is in the top tier - it doesn't have to be the most expensive, but you should definitely not be "on sale." It is unprofessional and never a good idea to undercut other teachers in the area with the same level of experience and education, even if you are trying to build up your numbers.

Coupons and Discounts
I have never offered coupons and I still do not offer sibling discounts until a family reaches three, then I start to feel like a discount would be mutually beneficial. I figure my time is not less valuable with the number of family members I am teaching, and they will value my expertise and availability more if they understand this. I do however offer incentives (5% pay in full discount IF you pay EARLY). I do this because I don't need to spend as much time on administrative costs or time and feel it is worth a small percentage of the tuition bill.

Median Community Age
Capitalize on the average age of people in your community. If you live in a place that has older people, be sure you are familiar with RMM (Recreational Music Making for Adults). If you have young children not old enough for private piano study, be sure you are familiar and offering early childhood music programs such as *Musikgarten, Music Together* or *Kindermusik*. Do you have a large high school population in your area? What about Recreational Music Making for teenagers? Log on to iTunes.com and start listening to the top 100! There are great options for age-appropriate music and curriculums.

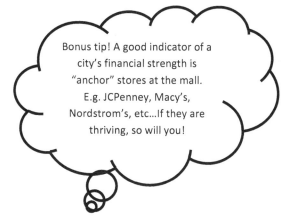

7 – IMAGE AND BRANDING

Centre for Musical Minds

Mission

I can honestly say I am on a mission to make music come alive for students, parents and teachers. I like to keep things fresh, fun; it keeps people wanting more. In a blog posted on www.hbr.org, Dan Pallotta asked, "Do you have a mission, or are you on a mission?" He then goes on to talk about how a person on a mission can be inspiring and exciting.

> "Steve Jobs is famous for having said 'I want to make a ding in the universe', Walt Disney, for having said of Disneyland, 'I just want it to look like nothing else in the world.' Springsteen said, 'More than anything else — more than fame or wealth or even happiness — I just wanted to be great.'"

> Now these are mission statements. They yearn. They cry. They're unequivocal. And they're the product of the soul — the product of a passion for living and building and creating. They're not the product of a writing exercise."

In the world of marketing and advertising, you need to be talked about. What will people say about you?

What is your mission? Have you communicated that mission clearly? And have you implemented it in ways that are easy to see ? If you don't already have a mission statement and can't think of something within 30 seconds, you probably aren't doing anything very innovative or earth-shattering. Time to define yourself as a musical educator and to determine your niche.

For what do you want to be known? Envision some of your students' parents having a conversation with another parent and they are talking about piano teachers. What would they be saying about you? Is this something for which you want to be known? If it is, run with it, market that very "thing" or message. If it isn't, then look at this as a wonderful opportunity to change and define what you and your teaching represent. If you have to spell out your mission, that probably means you are not "on a mission," which defeats the entire purpose of having one.

Marketing

When I started teaching out of my house in Frisco, I developed a HUGE word-of-mouth following from my city's online forum where I would post feedback when people asked about piano lessons. Keep in mind that word-of-mouth is great, but probably not enough if you want to keep numbers high. As an independent teacher, you need a constant flow of students and a waiting list. Supply and demand! The better the "supply" (that would be you), the more people want you...the more you can charge, the more students you have....get the picture? Get an ad out in a place where parents and students are reading. Are you on the search engines? Don't waste your money on the newspaper ad. People don't read those and, if they do, the one person you may get from the ad will hardly pay for the hundreds of dollars you had to pay to run just a few lines.

Brochures and business cards. Again, no home-printing! Take a look at VistaPrint.com or UPrinting.com. Call up your local printing company and see if they can do a price match from an online quote. If you don't trust yourself with an online program that allows you to choose colors, upload logos and include photos, then get a professional to design your materials for you. This is your image to the outside world, to the people who most likely don't know you personally. It's your image, your brand. What is the message you are trying to get across to prospective students? Once you determine this, make sure this is actually the message being received by potential clients! Helpful ideas for design come from questions you may ask yourself:

1. What are my target ages?
2. Do I want to be known as fun, serious or a combination?
3. What do I want to highlight about myself and my program?
4. Am I modern and serious, modern and fun, or reliably traditional?

Effective ways to get your "brand" out and "self-market" include:

1. Website! Website! Website! Sign your website up for Google AdWords (start with $30/month)
2. Contact local music teachers at school and see if you can do a demonstration or get listed on the school website
3. Fliers or direct mailings (This depends on your advertising budget.)
4. Offer incentives (not discounts) for current students to refer their friends (e.g. gift cards for current customer referrals)
5. Online Forums and Local Publications - work them!
6. Social Networking. Facebook page, LinkedIn, Twitter, YouTube are the essentials
7. Materials: Hand out your brochures to daycares, playgroups, churches and anywhere else that will accept them!

Make sure the image you are conveying to the public is consistent. Your brochures should match your website (and vice versa) as well as incorporate the same image/logo that is on your business card. ALWAYS have your logo! Here are some examples of various printed materials we currently have in circulation....

Beginner Assignment Sheet

Lesson Date: _____

Centre for Musical Minds

** Write in minutes of practice time for each day of the week. Mark a / for days you did not practice.

	M	T	W	T	F	S	S
Warm Up/Technique							
Activity Book p:							
Lesson Book p:							
p:							
p:							
p:							
Performance Pieces							

www.CentreforMusicalMinds.org

Beginner Assignment Sheet with Logo – essential for branding!

Musikgarten and PPK Summer Brochure - front and back
Appealing for a demographic that caters to young children…a great
marketing tool for preschools, mothers-day-out programs and young families.

May 14th 5pm

Centre for Musical Minds

Honors Recital
8048 Southmark Dr Frisco, 75035

Linnea Skold	Funkasaurus Eric Baumgartner	16th c. March Palmer and Lethco
Ava Colberg	The Rose Amanda McBroom, arr. Faber	Just Struttin' Along Martha Mier
Elaine Zheng	"First Term at the Piano" No. 15; Bela Bartok	Pagoda Bells William Gillock
Iniya Vidyashankar	A Swing Thing Eric Baumgartner	Pumpkin Boogie Nancy Faber
Sarah Hoving	Minuet in G Petzold/Bach	Phantom of the Opera Andrew Lloyd Weber, arr. by Faber
Anamika Suresh	Snake Charmer Nancy Faber	Beauty and the Beast from the motion picture, music by Alan Menken
Siri Potluri	Study Anton Diabelli	Drifting Clouds William Gillock
Priya Patel	Minuet in G Eric Baumgartner	Toccatina Dmitri Kabalevsky
Adam Cordeiro	Allegro con Fuoco Dvorak, arr. by Kraehenbuehl	Big Earl's Honky Tonk Blues Eric Baumgartner
Jacob Cordeiro	Prelude in C J.S. Bach	
Savonne Price	Sonatina in A Minor Alfred Benda	If I Ain't Got You Alicia Keyes
Adrian Andreescu	Sonatina Op. 36, No. 1 Muzio Clementi	The Matador Carolyn Miller

Students, thank you all for your hard work, dedication and musical tenacity!
Parents, your support is integral to your child's success and we thank you for
all of your hard work, dedication and continued support. It is a true joy to be able to work with such
wonderful families.

Sincerely,
CMM Faculty and Staff

For a traditional recital, this program is clean, consistent with logo and visually appealing!

Keeping student numbers up in a down economy
Published in Summer/Fall 2010 for MTAC Publication

"Often the difference between a successful person and a failure is not that one has better abilities or ideas, but the courage that one has to bet on one's ideas, to take a calculated risk - and to act."
Andre Malraux

Ah, "the economy". This seems to be the overwhelming response when people talk about numbers being down in comparison to anything prior to the most recent recession. This "the economy" response always comes in a more somber, lower tone of voice and refers to conference participation, domestic vehicle purchases, new home building. It could refer to fewer carrots at the grocery store if we let it. Mother Nature didn't cooperate because of (insert somber, lower voice here), "the economy." Numbers at Apple certainly aren't down, and dare I say, look at Amazon.com's profits from the last quarter....and so, we have to ask ourselves why. To me, it is plain and simple: People are loyal to what they trust, what they know works, and to what is innovative. In Apple's case, pretty packaging doesn't hurt either.

Welcome to our ever-changing new reality. Instead of thinking of the infamous economy as being down, I propose we take this as an opportunity to change our perception. Instead of the somber tone and lowered voice, it is time we view our economy as our reality. This is THE economy, not the "down" economy and we will embrace it with a sense of excitement and endless possibilities! The sooner we can grasp onto our "real" reality, the sooner we can get our studio numbers up, and keep them up regardless of the GDP.

> This is THE economy, not the "new" economy. Take this recent recession as an opportunity to evaluate yourself, your studio and your value system.

There is no question about it, consumers (your clients) are watching where they are spending their money, now more than I can ever recall. It is imperative you examine your studio from all angles, and determine what is and what is not working. Take this recent recession as an opportunity to evaluate yourself, your studio and your value system. Ask your best clients what it is about you, your studio and your personal musical values that make them want to stay involved. Once you determine that, ask the same valued clients "if there is one area of improvement you could see, what would you recommend?" Notice the boundary, just *one* area of improvement. You can thank me later.

Reflection is a good thing. I personally like to focus on positive reflection, and I particularly like to study what other people do that works. The good news happens when you take a look at Apple's sales - clearly people still have disposable income! When a consumer is buying a product that they trust and VALUE, they make the sacrifice and deem it a worthwhile purchase. If they like the result, they will tell their friends. When you are a teacher who has families who trust in you, relate to you, and VALUE you, they will be sure that their private music lessons are core to their lives, not optional. They will also tell their friends.

This brings me to my next point. It is your responsibility to communicate and instill an understanding in your clients that private music lessons are not optional. The question you should be asking yourself is: How can I make myself indispensable? Once you determine that, the next step is to articulate and implement how you will achieve your STRATEGY. Yes, I said Strategy! You as a music teacher need to have a strategy in how to retain students and add new ones over the coming year(s).

> Have a retention strategy. Survey the clients/families you value and find out exactly why they love you!

At the Music Teachers Association of California this past July, I had the privilege of sitting on a panel with pedagogical heavy-weights Dr. Scott McBride Smith, Lee Galloway, Michelle Sissler, Bonnie Blanchard, Brian Chung and Gary Ingle. When I began my spiel, I asked the audience how many teachers in the room had experienced growth in their studios this past year. Just as I thought, about 3/4 of the room raised their hand. Sound surprising to you? These are the innovators, the thinkers and the "shaker-uppers" that who have growth, not the people who keep doing what they are doing, hoping and expecting things to improve.

If you choose to "keep doing what you're doing" and change nothing, how can you expect your studio numbers to improve? Let us take a look at where you are. As an example, with 30 students on your roster, you would like to retain your 30 and gain 10. Create a 5-question survey about what your families like about lessons with you, and ask for one area of improvement. Show your client base you are listening to them, value their voice and take steps to show them that.

Once you know exactly why your families love you (or don't love you), implement a way to emphasize those qualities that make them want to stay with you. One of the main reasons my families love me is because I radiate positive honesty. I view all of my students as accomplished learners but make a point to not lie to them (e.g. saying "great" when it wasn't). I make them earn the "great" and they know exactly why. It's addictive, seeing progress and feeling it.

Once you know exactly why families love you, figure out what you can do to attract the same kinds of people (your favorite families!). Be sure you are giving incentives to people who recommend you. Everyone loves iTunes cards, t-shirts, gift cards...people love rewards. Just ask your students!

I may be criticized for saying this, but how you present yourself is very important. People like to be around other people who are attractive and fun. Buy a new pair of designer jeans and wear it with a professional looking top. A hip new tie or a pair of outrageous shoes will liven things up. For something easy, upgrade your look with a new office color, or add Guitar Hero to your waiting area. Imagine how many people will talk about THAT.

During the conference panel discussion, technology guru Michelle Sissler of *Keys to Imagination* talked about the importance of a niche, something that gives you an edge over the teacher with identical credentials and who is about five minutes away from your location. What makes you two different? What are you doing that makes you stand out and that makes a family want to be a part of your studio? Whatever decisions you make, be sure you are clearly communicating it to the general public and remember that it is **not** okay to undercut other music professionals in your area.

During that same panel, master teacher, Bonnie Blanchard talked about the importance of professionalism and of having fun; letting your inner enjoyment shine in everything you do. She discussed teaching all the non-musical habits and ideas that are so integral to success in life, but using music as her tool for the "positive corruption" of America's youth. Ms. Blanchard made it clear that the teacher sets the tone; from promptly responding to emails, scheduling, to setting boundaries and beyond. Her point is we must represent a level of quality in all that we do; from the way we dress to the way we end our lessons.

Seasoned pianist Lee Galloway addressed numbers, pure and simple. If the parents of students aren't getting a raise, do you think it is the wisest thing to raise your rates? Gone are the days where music educators can take an annual raise for granted, but we can embrace where we are and make the best of the situation.

RMM expert Brian Chung spoke about the importance of innovative, creative ways to boost student roster numbers. He advised tapping into the baby-boomer generation and focusing on gaining some adult students. To that, I ask readers to look at what kind of age demographics are in your area? How can you capitalize on those?

You are in a beautiful time in the development of your studio. This is an opportunity, an opportunity to determine what works and eliminate what doesn't. This is an opportunity to reacquaint yourself with what you do best. Instill the values that matter now and throughout the lives of your students. We seem to spend our whole lives trying to be just like all the others. Set yourself apart! Whatever you choose to do, please enjoy the journey you are on and look forward to the plan you set in motion to achieve your goals and dreams.

8 – SHOW ME THE MONEY

Two hard and fast rules I have learned about tuition:

1. Clients pay by semester, not month-to-month
2. Late payment (10 days) results in termination. Period. Not a late fee...termination. If the late-payer's employer didn't pay them for an extended period of time, they probably wouldn't show up to work. You shouldn't either.

The most important part: Money

Here are a handful of my rules when it comes to receiving payment:

1. There is no such thing as paying month-to-month; invoice by semester or year (with a monthly tuition installment option). You need to make it clear that your clients are not paying for the 30 or 45-minute lesson that week, they are paying for a service, knowledge base, your professional development, administrative fees, equipment, operational costs and your 401k. See

www.CentreforMusicalMinds.org and click on Resources, then Tuition for a great explanation!

2. Unlike a department store, I do not offer sales.

3. Promotions and thank-you's are great. Payment in full receives a 5% discount (since it is less hassle).

4. (Consistently late) Payments 10 days late result in lesson termination. Period. For the people who are normally on time I always give them the benefit of the doubt but be sure you are not a push-over.

5. Yes, credit card payments are necessary and no, you should not punish people for using them instead of writing a personal check.

> I recommend that the first service you outsource, when you are able, is that of bill collection or at the very least automate via software.

After my studio essentially 'blew up' -- I was teaching 75 private students out of my house -- I was so busy I could barely think straight. To curb some of the stress and workload, I hired my sister 1,000 miles away to handle the accounts receivable. She was essentially the "bill collector" and we did everything with email. She would correspond with people who were late in their tuition installments and she would implement fines. It is very difficult for the face of the teacher to be the face of the bill collector, for multiple reasons. I felt that, when I had that separation (which I still have), it was much less stressful and the parents were more respectful in the long run. Before I was simply using email invoices but now, I invoice using this fantastic program called Studio Helper. You might look into Musicians Helper as they are owned by the same company as Studio Helper but are more geared toward the independent teacher. Studio Helper has definitely helped my anxiety levels go down, and kept me organized! Another popular software is Jack Rabbit which is definitely worth a look.

Credit Cards

I personally have PayPal set up for my clients and recently set up Square where I can take credit cards for a nominal fee via my iPad or iPhone. There is no setup fee, no monthly fee and it took less than five minutes total. There is not a cart on my website, but simply a link from the invoice that automatically takes them to PayPal to fill the information in. I also do not charge a convenience fee, as when I use my card I expect the same courtesy at all businesses, small and large. I personally prefer to do business with establishments and people who accept credit card payments versus those who do not. When I made the decision to accept payments using credit cards, PayPal was the most economical way for me. It became a question of losing 2% of my fee or not getting paid on time and this is a decision that you need to make based on your principals. Checks, of course, are most often times a good way to keep track of payments, (yes, keep a record of which check number they give you) and though we all love cash, it is risky for reporting and recording purposes. A paper trail is always best.

What I find to be useful is to have a payment due date such as the 1st or 15th of each month, the month BEFORE. This way if you are not paid and the family "forgets to come," you can replace that student and hopefully not lose the revenue. Granted, if services were rendered, there was a prior payment agreement and you were not paid, that is a tax write-off in the business loss category....it's still better to have reliable revenue coming in!

BE FIRM. You have a policy for a reason, be sure to follow it! I'll say it again, one of my favorite things I did during my first year out of graduate school was to hire my sister as my the "bill collector" so I was only the face of the teacher. People were more respectful overall, and payments came in when they were supposed to. In the rare occasion someone did not pay on time, the 'late payment' notices were not from the teacher, but rather some third person implementing a policy that exists for a reason! Ingenious, isn't it?

If I had a second chance, I would keep better financial records from the start. Thankfully we always have bank statements to rely on, but being the numbers geek that I am, I like to see where the money comes from, where it goes and then how to break it down by percentages. As far as I can see, the gaping hole in independent music teaching is the financial aspect, which is at least half of what we do! If it isn't, it should be. What other business allows you to be so fluid and keep such loose records?

What makes you think your studio idea will be successful in a particular zip code?

The most definitive statements I could articulate that convinced me I could "make it" in Frisco, Texas, included these:

- There is a substantial need for a young educated piano teacher in the Frisco community.
- There was one music school in the city and only a dozen piano teachers in the local association.
- There is more business than the music school and 12 piano teachers could   handle.
- The current pedagogical trends were not being stretched to their best advantage in this area.
- Demographic projection was perfect for piano teaching.
- Frisco demographics exceeded national statistical averages in quality of life, median household income, average age of the city and projected growth

Business Plan

What business plan?! I'm a musician! Welcome to the American economy and the land of opportunity and entrepreneurship. If you own and operate a piano studio, or music studio of any sort, you need to know what it takes to make a business sustainable. To get any sort of financing or business loan, you need to have a plan that has been so well-thought-out that if you needed (or choose) to apply for a loan, the loan officer would grant you start-up money. Making your vision come true is so important and it takes an incredible amount of research and detail that you might spend an entire year preparing for your plan and have it rejected at several financial institutions just because they didn't like your writing style. The idea of a business plan is to capture important data that makes a positive impact on your audience whether it be yourself, family, a bank or a private investors. Highlight specific details that can be read swiftly and present them in a clear and concise way. Emphasize key points with charts and snapshots that can be backed up later in the document.

My favorite book on the market is *Successful Business Plan: Secrets & Strategies* written by Rhonda Abrams. For anyone accepting funding (from family, friends or otherwise), I cannot stress enough how important I feel it is for you to read this book.

When writing a plan, be sure the tone is straightforward, even understated. Let the information you convey (rather than your language) lead to the conclusion that your business will become successful. *Successful Business Plan: Secrets & Strategies* is an invaluable resource.

Whether you are considering starting an independent studio from scratch, considering expanding or upgrading your existing setup, or if you are planning to branch out into the land of music schools, you should always have a plan. As taken from Rhonda Abrams' book *Successful Business Plan: Secrets & Strategies,* when creating your plan, the following factors contribute most to your business and planning successes (p.3).
- The Business Concept
- Understanding the Market
- Industry Health and Trends
- Clear Strategic Position and Consistent Business Focus
- Capable Management
- Ability to Attract, Motivate and Retain Employees
- Financial Control
- Anticipating Change and Adaptability
- Company's Values and Integrity
- Responding to Global Opportunities and Trends

Your business plan should have a minimum of three years worked out with a budget and projected income. Whatever you do, be conservative on your income and overestimate your expenses. Don't pay someone to do this for you; you can and you should figure this out on your own!

A good business plan will include the following components:
1.0 Introduction
2.0 Executive Summary
3.0 General Business Description
4.0 Market Research and Analysis
    4.1 Ages of potential students and distribution in age
    4.2 Ethnic Backgrounds and effects
    4.3 Total market size
    4.4. Growth Trends
5.0 Competitive Analysis
    5.1 Don't forget your contingency plan!
6.0 Business Concept and Operational Plan
    6.1 This is where your description of the studio and marketing plan
        should be explained
7.0 Organization and Management

My personal business plan for when I upgraded to a commercial location was approximately seventeen pages. According to Rhonda Abrams in her book, *Successful Business Plan: Secrets & Strategies*, the length of your business plan should be 10 to 35 pages not including Financials and Appendices, and should cover three to five years worth of budget and cash flow projections. The whole point is to think through the thousands of dollars you will be hopefully be given, so that you have the ability and know-how to pay it back (with interest).

> "You must have ongoing contingency plans to allow for miscalculations, disappointments, and bad luck. It's assumed that if you're a leader, you don't make mistakes. But it's not so; if you're decisive, you'll sometimes miscalculate, and sometimes just be unlucky. You need to openly discuss the possibility of mistakes, so people are prepared and aren't crestfallen when they occur. You need to rehearse your contingency plans."
> *Bill Walsh Former Coach and President, S.F. 49ers*

Budget and Cash Flow Analysis
Recurring monthly costs to consider:
- Rental space/mortgage
- Billing/scheduling software
- Accounting software
- Electricity
- Internet (YouTube, LinkedIn, Facebook, Rhapsody and iTunes, need I say more?)
- Phone - your studio should have its own line
- Water dispenser/fountain for clients

- Referral incentives
- Web hosting
- Office supplies
- Music expenses
- Instrument payment
- Advertising
- Google AdWords
- Insurance

Once you have your expenses listed, determine how many students and at what price you need to maintain in order to meet your minimum. Then, figure out how much you would "like" to make and devise your strategy based on those concrete numbers. A business does not build overnight, but you can definitely begin to establish your name through networking groups, flyers and membership organizations. Advertising does not have to be a huge expense, but it does need to be incorporated if you want to build your business. The one regret I have when I transitioned from my home studio to my commercial location is that I should have allocated more revenue to advertising dollars for more upscale magazines and SEO optimization.

To even begin the process of securing funding from a financial institution, you will need to have a significant amount of paperwork ready. See list on the next page.

Getting the Loan
- SBA Loan Application
- Personal Background
- Personal Financial Statement (this means EVERYTHING)
- Business Financial Statements (Profit and Loss)
- Projected Financial Statements from the last three years
- Ownership and Affiliations
- Loan Application History
- Personal Tax Returns
- Business Tax Returns
- Resume
- Business Lease

You need a new instrument, larger teaching space and some gadgets. You want to apply for a Small Business Association (SBA) loan. An SBA loan is one that allocates up to $50,000 - anything over that amount is a (regular) business loan. Because of the tight lending market, what used to be a sure thing is no longer, and you must go into the bank prepared. What you need:

1. Outstanding Credit Score of well above 700
2. Three years financial history doing what you are doing
3. A rock solid business plan, which includes your contingency plan should something go wrong (you know, like the economy crashing)

Once you have compiled the necessary paperwork, it is imperative to set up a consultation at several different financial institutions to go over the possibilities. The process is very thorough, as you can see, but it is thorough for a reason. This is a lot of money! There are many people 'in business' that should not be because of poor management skills. Running a business takes a completely different skill set than teaching private music lessons!

Most business loans are fixed term which means you pay a specific amount each month for the life of the loan.

After the Plan So you have your business plan, and you are implementing it to a T. Pat yourself on the back; this is no small feat!

Come to terms with the fact now, that you have to constantly evaluate your business and its terms of operation. What works today may not work next year so never stop the improvement process. This includes your teaching artistry, your business plan, the implementation of your business plan and all things that may affect your tenure as CEO of your company. Make a point of subscribing to teaching magazines and attending conferences that will help inspire your teaching to be better. Do yourself a favor and keep current on leadership, entrepreneurship and economic trends that face our country. If you are not on top of it, who else will be?

Taxes
Let a qualified professional handle your legal and financial matters. When I say "qualified professional" I don't mean cookie cutter tax service (stay away from those), I mean find a reputable accountant or CPA and pay a couple hundred dollars to have it done correctly.

Spending Money
It all boils down to this: will my purchase make me money (generate revenue) or will I lose money? Not "if I buy this now, in four years will it make me money", but "if I purchase this product today will I begin making money on it in four weeks." Regardless of if the economy "gets worse" or "improves" - WILL THIS INVESTMENT MAKE YOU MONEY? Feel my point? An iPod will indirectly make you money, a computer can

potentially make you money and an iPad if used correctly, can make you money.

Additional Reading: Got Money? It's all about the Business Plan!
First published Spring 2011 for ComposeCreate.com

"Studies of business success over time have shown that companies that emphasize goals in addition to making money succeed better and survive longer than companies whose sole motivation is monetary." Rhonda Abrams, *The Successful Business Plan; Secrets & Strategies.*

As a seasoned piano teacher, you probably haven't thought to write up a business plan. You might be saying to yourself, "why do I need a business plan, that's for big companies." What we often forget is that we ARE a company. We may not be a large corporation, but we are certainly a business, however small. Each of us is also a brand, and there should be a plan with each brand! While a lot of business plans are for other people to secure funding, your plan (most likely) is for you to articulate your philosophy and mission, see how your expenses line up with your income, and identify solutions needed for any changes. During the construction of this in-depth analysis of your current studio, it will allow you to stay competitive in your market.

Knowing which direction you are heading gives you much more control on your future retirement. You plan and plan and plan for your students; take some time to plan for yourself.

Anyone who is teaching and providing an important part of a family's (if not sole) income should have a financial plan, not just a family budget. The plan itself does not have to be 75 pages, but rather between 15 and 20. You first need to assess the goals and purpose of your company. Yes you love teaching, but what is your philosophy that you embrace to reach your goals. What are your financial goals? How much are you actually spending on studio expenses? You know how much you deposited last month (or year), but what did you set aside for retirement and savings? This whole process will help your money-making potential!

A truly complete outline of a business plan will be composed of the following:

I. Executive Summary
II. Company Description
   A. Name
   B. Mission and Objectives
III. Industry Analysis and Trends
   A. Size of industry
   B. Industry Maturity
   C. Seasonal Factors
IV. Target Market
   A. Demographics! (I love these reports)
   B. Purchasing Patterns
   C. Disposable Income
V. The Competition
   A. Are there music schools nearby?
   B. Is your city saturated with independent teachers?
   C. How are you different?
   D. How will you remain valuable?
VI. Marketing Plan
   A. Your Message
   B. Strategy to brand yourself
   C. Strategic Partnerships
VII. Development
   A. Long-Term goals
   B. Growth Strategy (or maintenance strategy)
   C. Milestones
VIII. The Financials
   A. Income Statements
   B. Cash-Flow Projections
   C. Balance Sheet

None of this is rocket science, but it does force you to get organized, to articulate who you are and what you do and to evaluate where you are financially. It can also lead you to where you want to go.

9 – TEACHING SPACE AND IMAGE

The Instrument

For those of you who have never purchased an instrument without the guidance of a professional (especially pianists), please listen carefully to what I am about to tell you.

I made a colossal (as in $12,500) mistake in buying an absolutely horrible instrument, that I didn't even know was horrible. I suppose my piano shopping was probably similar to me going out car shopping. "Well, it has 4 wheels, it has doors, a radio and it runs, what more can a girl ask for?" Let's just say on round two of both piano and car buying, I made much better, informed choices!

The colossal $12,500 mistake.

What the instrument did do for me was get me talked about - not everyone has a grand piano to teach on and it is impressive to most people. I bought a horrible instrument that I didn't even know was horrible. I lived to tell the tale, as it were, and did much better my second time around. However, what that first beastly instrument DID do for me was get me talked about - not everyone has a grand piano to teach on and it is impressive to most people.

So the question is: Is it imperative to have a quality grand piano or will an upright do? The answer lies in the question, how seriously do you want to be taken? My opinion is a resounding YES. As in, you need a grand piano! It is a worthy investment. You will attract a more serious student certainly, and people who value you AND your equipment. Teaching on your grandmother's old upright is probably not the wisest decision. If you are choosing between two dentists, are you going to go with the dentist flashing the pearly whites or the one with the coffee-stained off-white teeth? I'll discuss how you can pay for that nice grand piano later. But for now, suffice it to say that you need to invest in your business and this is definitely a worthy investment!

Your teaching space
Keep it simple, keep it clean and make it welcoming. Time and time again I am complimented on my teaching space. When I was in my home studio people walked in the door to a beautiful grand piano and a clean, spacious learning environment. Your teaching space should always be picked up, vacuumed, dusted, smelling pleasant (not overwhelming) and give the appearance of organization. It should not remind them of a used (cluttered, though charming) bookstore. Organized piles are okay, but a filing system is better, for multiple reasons. Most people I know who earn six-figure incomes are nicely dressed - sometimes in suits, sometimes in designer jeans.

Business Cards - Do not skimp on the business cards - please do not print them from your home printer! Spend the money and have nice cards designed and printed for you. Or, do it yourself online with numerous websites dedicated to consumers uploading their work and submitting it for print. When it's all said and done, the cost of having a professional printer print your cards will most likely be less than all that you have spent on ink and expensive business card paper.

Headshots – For my first website, I had nice photos taken by a friend – and they were free! It is a wonderful investment however, even if you do have to pay someone. You will be using them on your website and even on your business cards; be sure to look sharp. I recently had professional photos taken in McKinney (near Dallas) Texas, and paid $125. I keep the images on a CD and have the freedom to use them at my discretion for all promotional purposes. Professional photographs should not cost an arm and a leg, just a finger. See the following pages for examples. The combination of the two photos creates a nice mix, but Option B looks much more appealing when you add Option A in there…certainly for a website.

Option A

$125 investment in head shots paid off! To me, this look says "fun" and "current". Statement made.

Option B

Louise Goss and me at NCKP 2009 – A teaching legend but the photo could not be stand-alone material in promotional pieces. Why? I would need to introduce both of us and, in the process, take the focus away my business.

This photo would not help me establish a reputation but would strengthens an already-solid one.

Social Networking

Please tell me your studio has a Facebook page. If you do not, go to www.facebook.com and register for one, TODAY! Then, invite all of your piano students and parents to be part of your group where you can add videos, post recital announcements, post studio news. It's a wonderful way to keep your students, parents and "studio family" connected. Not everyone is on Facebook, but I would guess that the majority of your client base is. Additionally, I would hope you have a LinkedIn page, to highlight your professional accomplishments. It's like a digital CV.

Correspondence

I have not found a significant need for personalized stationary but I have found a need for a signature line at the conclusion of an email that gives ALL of my contact information. E.g.

Kristin Yost
Executive Director, The Centre for Musical Minds
w. www.CentreforMusicalMinds.org
t. 214.123.4567
e. exdir@centremm.org
skype. CentreforMusicalMinds

There is nothing more frustrating than when you want to contact someone and you don't have their information at your fingertips - in many cases it means you either get the student, or you don't. Face it - we live in such a fast-paced world and the last thing people want to do is spend time looking for another phone number or for another service. Make it easy!

10 - LOGISTICS OF SIX FIGURES

> Summertime...set your expectations high.
> Expect half to balk at the very thought of a
> summer requirement. Offer something for
> everyone, including traveling families. Group
> classes, camps, and minimal (though longer)
> private lessons come to mind.

You need 12 months of revenue, period. If you don't have the revenue in the summer, you will never make the six-figure mark, or even come close. Your summer expectations need to be set high, and expect half to balk at the very thought of a summer requirement. Expect half and hope that three/fourths enroll. Operate from the mindset of "what I offer is an experience you cannot receive anywhere else" and offer something for everyone, including the families that travel the majority of the summer. Group classes, camps and minimal private lessons come to mind. Since the children are not in school during summer months, utilize their open schedules and create a new (flexible) schedule that allows for exploration, learning, creativity and enjoyment. Who wouldn't want to pay for that?

I don't want to tell you how to do things, but I do want to give you an idea of what I do - it works very well for me and I re-evaluate each year. Here is an example of a payment calendar based on 30-minute lessons.

Months and lessons	Payment	Amount
August - 2	August 1	$120
September - 4	September 1	$120
October - 4	October 1	$120
November - 3	November 1	$120
December - 3	December 1	$120
January - 3	January 1	$120
February - 4	February 1	$120
March - 3	March 1	$120
April - 3	April 1	$120
May - 2/Flex	May 1	$120
June - Flex	June 1	$120
July - Flex	July 1	$120

I do offer incentives to pay in advance (5%) during the spring, but no sibling discounts unless there are three of them. I divide my year into three semesters:

Fall - mid/end of August through December
Spring - January through mid-May
Summer - mid/end of May through August 1

For more information, please visit www.CentreforMusicalMinds.org to see the specifics.

Summer

For those of you who like time off, you really need to teach, at least a little bit! Each summer since 2006 I have done something different. I have yet to find my 'perfect summer' schedule but each summer gets me just a little closer. I have done the extremes: 90% camps/groups and 10% private lessons. 10% camps and 90% private lessons...this year I am aiming for 65% private lessons, 35% group classes. When taught correctly, group classes have such a wonderful social impact on students and the camaraderie is what keeps them involved and looking forward to group activities.

Because of the flexibility in many schedules, I try to encourage groups (okay, I mandate them) where we offer Music History, African Drumming, Basic CD Production using GarageBand, Song-writing, Music Theory, How to Make a Music Video, World Music, Mylie Cyrus singing and dancing and others. This year I am going to offer more private lesson options as I am wanting to have more forward motion. I have also implemented a summer "Keyboard Jam" which I hope will motivate and inspire the students during their months off of school. No homework = more practice, right?

How to get 12 Months of Revenue as an Independent Music Teacher
First published Spring 2011 for ComposeCreate.com

Are you tired of not making enough money, especially in the summer? Or are you perpetually frustrated because you think you should be making more, especially for all of the hours you put in? Well, let's figure out a way to fix that for you! Repeatedly I am asked how much I charge for summer, what I offer, and what I do for makeup lessons, My responses are all based on the school of 'hard knocks' because, chances are, they are not original ideas but modified based on what worked (and what didn't) the previous year. I had to figure all this out the hard way initially, but I have finally found a way that -- fingers crossed -- I think everyone should adopt! As readers probably know by now, I teach piano for my livelihood, not as a second income or just for fun. This is how my mortgage gets paid, how all of my bills are met and where my retirement goes (or grows). I need money coming in 12 months out of the year, and summer is not an option, period.

Piano teaching is a business, and one of your primary financial goals is to create a 12-month revenue stream, whether you realize it or not. There are months where you collect more, and months that are not as fruitful but the constant should be more money coming in, twelve months out of the year. There is no reason you should be forced to accept anything less. What we do at the *Centre for Musical Minds* is have an 11-month tuition revenue stream and in July we have an annual enrollment fee which covers music and recital fees - this amount is the same as 30-minute tuition and due in one lump sum. One of the reasons I have the enrollment fee due in July is because I take care of all of the music ordering for each student and supply books when they need them. Each summer I take advantage of 20-40% print music discounts for bulk orders. The enrollment fee is non-refundable and is prorated according to when students begin their study with us. A student who begins lessons in December is not going to pay the full amount upon enrollment and then again six months later.

Let's say as an example, you have 30 teaching hours each week, at the equivalent of $60/teaching hour ($120 monthly tuition) and at $1,800 per week, on average $7,200 per month, this is $86,400 annually. How can you collect $7,200 each month, even in the summer?

The reality of our lives is that our enrollment will go down a bit for summer, but it should not be drastically different. At the Centre, we have 36 to 38 billable tuition weeks. Each tuition installment is due on the 1st of each month, one month in advance. Fall and Spring semesters are sixteen weeks, and for summer instead of 30-minute lessons weekly, we require either six 45-minute lessons with three ninety-minute group sessions OR a week of music camp (three hours per day) plus four 45-minute private lessons. Summer monthly tuition price is the same as the Spring/Fall 30-minute price and would be equivalent to $360 for the summer package, versus the Fall/Spring 30-minute lesson price in full of $120.00 So, it looks like this (according to our numbers above):

August 1 through March 1 - tuition installments of $120.00 toward fall and spring semesters

April 1 through June 1 - tuition installments of $120 toward summer package

July 1 - $120 annual enrollment fee to cover the cost of music and recitals throughout the year

Per student, that is $1,440 annually. If you only taught 30-minute lessons, teaching 30 hours per week, that is $86,400. At 20 hours per week, that is $56,700. Even with the 30-teaching hours, this still allows for 2 or so hours a day for administrative work (when needed) and keeps you at a 40-hour work week. For some of you that may be too many teaching hours but for me, I personally prefer to work those hours in order to be able to hire someone to handle the things I do not particularly enjoy doing (like Quick Books entry!). That, and I want to be able to take vacations, get my house cleaned now and again and still have a savings account. Another way to curb excess lessons, is to only offer 45-minute lessons, in which case tuition would be higher, and you can allocate hours/dollars accordingly. Earning $80,000 a year isn't too bad is it! Even after taxes, that is well above the national average of $50,000 (www.Census.gov). Our jobs are relatively low stress, job satisfaction is extremely high and if communicated correctly, policies should be relatively simple to enforce. Sounds pretty great to me!

In order to maintain your studio numbers and participation, you need to make your families understand you are the best, and it's important for them to continue study year-round for their interest and satisfaction levels to stay up. With that, you will see your numbers stay relatively stable through summer. Now, what do you do about the families who say they would like to take the summer off but they still want their spot for fall, or for the families that leave for the summer? Not to worry, I have some ideas on that too!

1. Since Spring is so much longer, we start our 'summer' with three weeks of school remaining, so families who travel can be accommodated.
2. In order to keep placement for fall and not participate in summer, we require payment in full for the annual enrollment fee and fall, due April 1st and of course is non-refundable should they choose not to continue. This past week we had a record number of families pay for the year in full.

Going into summer is always a little tricky because you are bound to lose a few students. However, it doesn't mean you have to eat noodles for 3 months. Another creative idea I have used is instead of infusing pay-in-full discounts during the late summer/early fall, I moved it to Spring. This enables a music teacher to go into summer with a financial cushion and reallocate revenue for when it's truly needed.

So let's recap some of the important points to keep in mind for our 12-month revenue plan:

- Invoice by semester, NOT by the week or month

- Families on the monthly tuition plan should be paying one month in advance, NOT on the first of the month, for that month. This protects you.

- For the 12th month (July), have the annual enrollment fee due.

- Summer is not optional, but make sure you offer something of perceived additional value so you can keep tuition at the same rate. Offer a pay-in-full discount in the spring, versus the fall, to infuse some cash into your summer months bank account

POSTLUDE

So tell me, why is it you want to make more money? What will you do with it? Like the prelude says, have a plan. When you get this additional money, where will it go? How will you measure your bank account progress? Plan a trip, increase your savings, start a retirement fund, or purchase a new instrument....whatever you do, have a plan.

Your future bank balance is determined not by this book, but by the **opinion** of yourself and whether you feel you can make more money. Take the information from this book and use it to your advantage. Life is made up of facts and opinions. It's as simple as that, and I have given you the facts that made up my reality, which in turn are my opinions. If you want to change your bank account balance, then you need to examine your personal facts and develop your personal and professional strategy to make it better. If it does not happen right away, and you still believe in yourself and you are of the opinion that you **can** do this, then keep plugging away, being sure to evaluate your vision and your implementation of that vision. What about your actions is NOT working?

If you are starting your very first independent studio, or expanding from your home studio into something else, this book should provide you with valuable information to use on several different levels. Ultimately though, you need to educate yourself through mentors, books, more mentors and more books, and by your own intuition.

The natural progression of things, however, is going to be you finish reading this book, becoming wildly inspired. You get on a mission and you have a bank account which becomes more comfortable as you implement that mission.

> What I did that differs from 90%
> of the other music studios
> around me was that I have
> ALWAYS had a strategy. I put
> my goals first, and let my
> mission lead me to make
> strategic decisions.

My drive for quality education with quality instruments created a passionate within me that needed to be unleashed. What I did that differs from 90% of the other music studios around me was that I have ALWAYS had a strategy. I put my goals first and let my mission lead me to make strategic decisions. When you begin to put your mission first, your passion for learning and being the best teacher you can be, is elevated. If you don't have a passion for this and feel like you are not on a mission, it may be time to re-evaluate this independent music teacher career path. It may not be what you really want.

This might not happen right away, but it might happen eventually: your passion will die. And your business will follow suit. Typically a decline in a business happens in one of two ways: lack of business system and operation, or lack of passion. Having passion about something for me was involuntary, but in order to feed and keep it alive, I had to educate myself on the numbers of what it would take to make my passion a reality and keep it there.

What I created through my own passion was a place where learning became exciting. It was not the "same old stuff"....teacher sits at the bench for 30 minutes, gets out the pencil and highlighter, writes what the student does wrong, and the student leaves the lesson not really wanting to go back...but he or she does, because parents make them. What I did was create an environment that children WANT to come and learn in. The students, the parents, and the families are excited about learning, and wanted to learn more. The best part? Right now I am creating jobs, living out my passion and truly enjoying the journey I set in motion.

For new teachers - my advice to you
Find a mentor, someone who has gone through the process of being an independent music teacher. Your mentor provides a built-in knowledge and experience base that you (and I) are still working to acquire. And at different points in your life, you will require different mentors. Keep your eyes and mind open for another mentor to come into your life, someone who brings yet another perspective to your life.

See more of my thoughts about mentoring later in this chapter, under the heading *Life after graduate school: The importance of a Mentor*

While I offer encouragement about mentoring to new teachers, this chapter would not be complete without my offering a warning to them as well. Here it is: Remaining uneducated in basic business and financial practice is EXTREMELY risky if you are going to be self-employed. You are the CEO of your own company! Take my financial chapter and learn from my experience. My home studio is where I went through my first year as a full-time piano teacher. My home studio is where I learned the failures of what I did not want to make into habits. Remember and take this to heart: failure is a means by which to measure progress. Without failure, success does not exist.

If independent music lessons is the career path you choose, even in light of the previous caution, and you are in your early stages of opening up a studio, here are some rules I suggest you follow:

- You absolutely cannot live in an apartment. If you cannot or do not want to buy a house, rent one. When you have shared walls, you encounter problems that any   musician cannot avoid...don't do it. Besides, apartments have stricter   stipulations on business that can be conducted on their property as compared to   a Home Owners Association.

- Right off the bat, get a great instrument - it's called street credibility and a guarantee to attract the 'right' kind of students. Your dentist most likely does not have crooked, stained yellow teeth, right?

- Get certified. No other profession allows their members to NOT be certified, why should we? When was the last time you saw a school advertising for "uncertified" teachers? Or would you even consider going to a doctor who was not certified? Degrees are not enough anymore, this is part of the game.

- Hire someone to collect tuition - yes, "tuition". Get your high-school-aged nieces/nephews to do it, or a neighbor and pay them something for their time. All it takes is a few hours per month to send out client invoices/bills, email reminders, whatever you choose to do. Bottom line is there is someone holding your client accountable. You are the face of the teacher, and too often will be pressed to "be gracious". "Oh I forgot my checkbook this week, is it okay to pay you next week?" gets really old, really fast. Imagine their reaction if the company they worked for said that to them - oops, our computer with the accounts payable is broken...would it be okay to pay you next week?" I don't think so.

First year - "Must Do" List
Living accommodations: no shared walls!
Instrument: Grand Piano
Hire a "Billing Specialist"

Centre for Musical Minds, LLC

My current company is called Centre for Musical Minds. The Centre's philosophy is that we believe there is music in every person, and that all people, through music, can become happier, more confident and more creative human beings. At the Centre for Musical Minds, our mission is to provide a warm and supportive environment in which all students can explore the world of music with confidence and joy. Please check out the website at CentreforMusicalMinds.org and read more about what my first year of teaching taught me!

Current Economic Downturn

Of course the economic downturn is affecting us as music teachers. Regardless of political change, we are still a nation at war. Numbers at Apple certainly aren't down, and dare I say, look at their profits from the last quarter....and so, we have to ask ourselves why. To me it is plain and simple: People are loyal to what they trust, what they know works, and innovation. In Apple's case, pretty packaging doesn't hurt either.

Welcome to our ever-changing new reality. Instead of thinking of the infamous economy as being down, I propose we take this as an opportunity to change our perception. Instead of the somber tone and lower voice, it is time we view our economy as our reality. This is THE economy, not the "down" economy and we will embrace it with a sense of excitement and endless possibilities! The sooner we can grasp onto our "real" reality, the sooner we can get our studio numbers up, and keep them up regardless of the GDP.

There is no question about it, consumers (your clients) are watching where they are spending their money, more now than I can ever recall. It is imperative you examine your studio from all angles, and determine what is and what is not working. Take this recent recession as an opportunity to evaluate yourself, your studio and your value system. Ask your best clients what it is about you, your studio and your personal musical values that make them want to stay involved. Once you determine that, ask the same valued clients "if there is one area of improvement you could see, what would you recommend?" Notice the boundary, just one area of improvement. You can thank me later.

Between WWI and WWII, Americans made a point to define themselves as something completely different than Europe. Post WWII, there was a genuine sense of conservatism and wanting to give back to the betterment of society. There was a rise in the vernacular and concentration on American style - it is 2011 and I feel we are in a state of transition, with the obvious focus being more of a global emphasis. A prime example of success is after WWI when black intellectuals decided to approach the arts with a different idea; they presented western European ideas with African American traditions to demonstrate how it works together. It's not a question of one or the other. It's not about creating a new tradition, it's about mixing traditions and creating something we can call our own.

KRISTIN K. YOST

Life after graduate school: The importance of a Mentor
First appeared in Clavier Companion Winter 2011

"Listening, not imitation, is the sincerest form of flattery" ~ *Dr. Joyce Brothers*

You did it. You graduated! For the past six to seven years of your life you dedicated your time to studying, earning good grades, and establishing professional and personal relationships to last a lifetime. You practiced countless hours, probably took hundreds of tests in one form or another, learned your craft, and had a lot of fun. Now you are ready to move forward with your life. Your goal over these years in school has been to become "better." You studied to be a better pianist, a better student, a better musician, better theorist, and, hopefully, a better teacher. You graduated; now the fun begins! You can put everything you learned in the classroom into practice. Your effective teaching will draw in the "right" kind of students (talented and hard-working), and your love of music theory will be felt and appreciated by each and every one of your students. You will be a leader in your field!

The problems of reality

The above scenario would be great, but reality is quick to step in and say "Not so fast!" The past few years you have spent your professional career thinking, evaluating, and "practicing" for real life. You can hypothesize, reflect, theorize, and live life in the academic bubble all you want, but it is a bit more challenging that you thought. There are no textbook explanations for how you will make a living. You need to teach on an instrument like you used to practice on at the university, but nobody taught you how to acquire the money to purchase it. None of your classes covered how to handle the parent that hasn't yet paid you, though each week contains a promise to bring the checkbook next time. And what do you practice now that you are no longer preparing for a jury or recital? You are eager to apply everything you learned in school, but you are quickly learning that real life presents some surprising challenges.

For those of us who went into the private, independent teaching sector, there are many complex financial and human problems that, rest assured, will arise. The best thing you can do for yourself after graduation is to find and establish a relationship with a person you respect. It's easy to have a mentor while you're in school because of accessibility, so have several! It may be more important, however, to have a mentor after you leave the comforts of college. Whether this is a mentor from an actual mentoring program or simply someone who in your mind holds the winning pieces, make it a priority to make and keep a connection to someone who lives a life to which you aspire.

As noted in *The Harvard Business Review,* "Ever since the Greek poet Homer's 'faithful and wise' Mentor first advised Odysseus, or Merlyn the young King Arthur, wise men have counseled, taught, coached, and sponsored the young. There have been mentors and protégés in philosophy, the arts and letters, the military, and even in professional sports."
Mentoring speeds advancement in leadership and helps to fill gaps that you don't read about in your textbooks and musical scores.

Your mentor provides a built-in knowledge and experience base that you (and I) are still working to acquire. At this point in my life, I need something different than what I needed in school. It is healthy to learn and take what you can while still keeping your eyes and mind open for another mentor to come into your life. Someone who brings yet another perspective or area of expertise.

Finding a mentor

So where can you find these mentors? A mentor is not someone who necessarily wears a "I AM A MENTOR" t-shirt to the mall, nor is it someone with whom you always have a formal agreement. You are in search of and need someone to nurture and inspire you professionally as well as personally. Let us look at a couple of the obvious places: music teacher associations, perhaps an experienced teacher from your local association or someone whom you met at NCKP or MTNA. You may be inspired by an author you met at a book club meeting, or possibly by a neighbor who has been successful at her chosen profession. It could be someone from a church group or an extended family member. What about your parents, or maybe even a grandparent? A mentor can be someone who has a completely different profession, but who can provide insight and information to inspire and provoke a "do better" attitude.

I can personally think of many outstanding mentors I have had in my life, none of which signed a contract. With each of them not only did I observe problem-solving skills, mannerisms, fashion, and language, but I also asked questions about life, family, and personal habits. I remember my high school band director, Dennis Tischhauser, who transformed my self-image and in turn gave me hope for being "better." He saw me as an accomplished learner. He introduced me to my high school youth symphony conductor, Phil Scales.

69

This man gave up his Saturdays August through May, and his family vacation in June for the greater good of hundreds of high school students who have been profoundly changed by the opportunities he provided.

Were it not for these first two mentors, I would not be writing this article today, and I most certainly would not have gone to college as a music major. I remember my first collegiate piano professor, Dr. Rick Andrews, who planted the notion of graduate school in my head. I am the only person on both sides of my immediate family who has completed a college degree, let alone a graduate diploma. When I transferred from Augustana College to the University of Wisconsin-Eau Claire, Dr. Donald Patterson was the transformative teacher who taught me to love music and embrace my abilities. Because of my two collegiate piano instructors, I moved to Dallas in order to be trained by Mr. Alfred Mouledous. Every one of these mentors profoundly influenced me as a musician, but, more importantly, as a person. Are these people still my mentors? Not actively, but they have a presence in my life and I have their contact information should I need them again!

A multitude of mentors

After college, the most important people in my life have been primarily financial and education mentors (I figured I had the music thing under control by now, or at least manageable), and experienced private teachers with an array of expertise. Through diverse activities and wonderful parents with whom I interact each week, I have a well-rounded set of mentors. Some of them may not even realize they are my mentors! I keep these people on speed dial and make a point to regularly speak about the 'mundane' (which should never be underestimated) day-to-day life experiences as well as the important situations and ideas that have given me strong emotional reactions. It is these people whose advice, knowledge and friendship I seek and value. What I give them in return is a sense of hope, adventure, a way to stay sharp and actively engaging, and, most importantly, a friendship that they know will endure any business decision or endeavor that we discuss.

We all have students who ask an inordinate amount of questions (musical or otherwise), but they are not without purpose. I imagine in these lessons you also ask thoughtful, thought-provoking questions to challenge your student. These students are looking to you as one of their life mentors. Eric Booth dedicates chapter 14 of his book, *The Music Teaching Artist's Bible* to mentoring and says, "Good mentoring is more about asking great questions than telling great stories."

A role model, a mentor, a teacher of life … call us what they will - music educators are influential in so many ways! We are teaching our students about attention to details, creative expression, and self-assessment among other things. It would be naive to think that our students only come to learn about notes, rhythms, and new pieces. It would also be a disservice to not give them an emotional connection and safe place to think outside the box. So much of the fun stick-to-it-ness and learning that takes place in lessons is because our students love us first and foremost as members of their inner circle, as (potential) life mentors. We as piano teachers deliver the human element that makes wonderful, memorable experiences we hope the students can transfer into math studies, tae-kwon-do lessons, and quiet time with family for years to come.

Who in your life influences you, and how? I would like to challenge each of you to identify the mentors in your lives and reflect on why these people have had a profound influence. Once you do that, reach out and (if possible) thank them for being in your life. For those educators freshly out of school, be sure you find people who influences your learning and spend time with them. What makes them tick? How did they become successful? Finding mentors can prove to be challenging, because the mentor has to want to be a part of your life. You can always read texts, articles, magazines, books, or dissertations and identify with a person that way, which of course provides many benefits, but that lacks the human contact. The best mentors are the best listeners, those who ask the best questions.

As Eric Booth says, "Mentoring is the performing art that creates the future of our art, one deep relationship at a time."

ABOUT THE AUTHOR

Kristin K. Yost is the founder and executive director at the Centre for Musical Minds in Frisco, Texas. She is also the co-founder of PianoTeacherSchool.com and maintains an active workshop schedule at the national level; her areas of professional expertise include music business for independent teachers and practical application of technology in student lessons. Ms. Yost has been featured in the *American Music Teacher, Clavier Companion, Music Teachers Association of California Journal* and ComposeCreate.com. She is a highly sought-after teacher in the Dallas area and has students who have won regional and local competitions in classical as well as popular-music festivals.

To learn more about Ms. Yost, please visit CentreforMusicalMinds.org or PianoTeacherSchool.com.

Made in the USA
Lexington, KY
05 November 2012